The Stuff Dreams Are Made Of

The Art and Design of
Frederick and Louise Coates

Frederick and Louise Coates (centre)
examining one of their scrapbooks.

The Stuff Dreams Are Made Of

The Art and Design of Frederick and Louise Coates

AN EXHIBITION IN THE
THOMAS FISHER RARE BOOK LIBRARY
UNIVERSITY OF TORONTO
16 JANUARY – 27 MARCH 1997

ISBN 0-7727-6024-1

COVER: The design for the Hart House Theatre mural illustrating Shakespeare's *The Tempest*.

Printed and bound in Canada

Publication of this catalogue has been made possible by funding from the Friends of the Thomas Fisher Rare Book Library, Bell Canada, and Wentworth Walker.

Bell

Foreword

The Thomas Fisher Rare Book Library is delighted to present a record of the lives and artistic accomplishments of Fred Coates (1890-1965) and Louise Brown Coates (1889-1975). This exhibition rediscovers the art and design of Fred and Louise Coates for another generation of Canadians. It evokes a period when the Arts and Crafts movement not only influenced their art but also permeated all aspects of their lives. Their impressive house on Chine Drive was built in the Arts and Crafts tradition and stands today as a fine example of that tradition.

The wealth of photographs and sketchbooks, including many stage and costume designs, drawn mainly from the Fred Coates papers in the University of Toronto Archives, provide vivid impressions of the Coates. Pictures of the artists at work, the construction of their home, Sherwood, and the costume soirees held in Sherwood convey lasting impressions of their lives and, more generally, an artist's lifestyle in Toronto between the two World Wars. The exhibition also documents their artistic achievements with designs for architecture, graphics, theatre sets and costumes and it includes watercolours, drawings, photographs and objects illustrating these designers' long and varied careers.

On behalf of the Fisher Rare Book Library I want to thank Bell Canada, Wentworth Walker and the Friends of Fisher for funding this catalogue.

RICHARD LANDON
Director, Thomas Fisher Rare Book Library

Acknowledgements

6 • This exhibition is based on materials found in the Fred Coates papers housed in the University of Toronto Archives, including sketchbooks, photographs, and stage and costume designs. There also exists a small number of materials relating to Louise Brown Coates, who was also an artist in her own right. Because of the collaborative nature of many of the projects Fred was involved with, we decided to make this exhibition about both Fred and Louise.

The present publication and exhibition grew out of a smaller exhibition on Fred Coates, held in January 1996 at the Justina Barnicke Gallery at Hart House, University of Toronto. For help on that exhibition, I am grateful to numerous individuals including Dr. Thomas Howarth, Judy Schwartz, Sam Harris, Hrag Vartanian, Jan Bessy, Sara Nunes, Sasha Havelik, Galia Almagor, John Belle, Gary Donais, Ian and the late Margaret Forrest, Stan Kent, Hripsime Vartanian and Mindy Laxer.

This project could not have been undertaken without the support and help of many individuals, including the current owners of the Coates house in Scarborough, as well as the long time friends of the Coates, including Les and Bernice Campbell, Don and Mary Stangroom, Herb and Mary Harvey, Pim and Debi Schryer, who shared their memories of Fred and Louise and who loaned materials for the exhibition. I am grateful to John Belle and Gary Donais; to Paul Crouch and Karen Gray; to Neil McDonald, who kindly loaned us materials on Fred

and Louise from his collection; and also to the Layng   • 7
family for their loan and gift of material relating to the
Coates family. To Dr. Thomas Howarth, I owe a special
debt of gratitude, not only for the loan of his works and
images relating to Fred Coates, but also for his insight
regarding Fred's life and work.

I am grateful to Maureen Morin, who undertook the
digital scanning; to Richard Miller, who designed the
catalogue; and to Emrys Evans and Linda Joy, who
mounted the exhibition. The staff of the University of
Toronto Archives has been helpful throughout all phases
of the exhibition, especially Harold Averill, who first
introduced me to the Fred Coates papers at the
University Archives and shared his research on the
history of amateur theatre at the University of Toronto.
Finally, I would like to thank Hrag Vartanian for his
contribution to the catalogue and exhibition, his assistance on all aspects of the exhibition, as well as for his
essay on Chine Drive which provides a context for the
house, the street, and the community. In closing I would
like to thank Gayle Garlock, for his full support and
encouragement throughout all phases of the exhibition
and the catalogue.

PAUL MAKOVSKY

THE ARCHIVE IS A REPOSITORY OF TEXTS,

Fred and Louise Coates.

FROM THE HOME,

Sherwood, the Coates's house on Chine Drive in Scarborough.

10

A scene from Faust *performed at the*
Hart House Theatre (1932).

Frances Loring (left) *and Louise Brown during their Washington trip (1913).*

FROM THE KNOWN,

Fred and Louise Coates.

TO THE UNKNOWN.

The Coates Family home in Nottingham (1912).

Foundations

PAUL MAKOVSKY

FREDERICK COATES WAS BORN 27 September 1890
in Nottingham, England, the son of Frederick Charles
and Abigail Dexter Coates. Little is known about his
early life. He grew up in a middle-class English family,
the eldest of four children, his sisters were named Vera,
Ida and Lin. A series of photographs taken in 1912,
depicts the Coates family and their two-storey Victorian
house, which was located on a private road on the
Mount in Nottingham. The family portrait taken in front
of the house reveals his Edwardian upbringing. At one
end, Fred's father, Frederick Charles, pushes a lawn
roller. His youngest sister looks at him, holding a lawn
tennis racquet. Another sister pauses from reading a
book. Fred's mother, Abigail, sits in a chair with a cup of
tea. Fred and a sister lounge on a garden bench. The
dining room and sitting room suggest an eclectic but
modest taste; with a mixture of styles in its furniture,
wallpaper and bric-a-brac.

The son of a chemist, Fred Coates became an artist
against his father's wishes. According to one account,
after Fred had mixed chemicals with reckless abandon
and dangerous consequences, his father suggested that he
might as well get on with his drawing, and gave him
permission to go to art school. Fred attended the
Nottingham School of Art around 1909, where he took
courses in drawing and architectural history. In 1910, he
travelled to Paris, which, since the 1880s, had become
the undisputed centre of sculptural activity. Fred visited

tourist sites and studied the classical and Beaux-Arts sculpture at the Louvre and at the Tuileries gardens. Little is known of Fred's stay in Paris, apart from a photo album of the sites, and his mention that he was constantly starving for food.

By 1911, he had enrolled in the Royal College of Art (RCA) in London, where he received three years of instruction in sculpture and modelling in the space of a year, graduating as a sculptor. He received a bronze medal for a design of a bronze panel. Only a few works survive from his period as a sculptor. A plaster relief of a mantel depicting the death of Socrates was exhibited at the RCA, and reflects his Beaux-Arts training, which is characterized by a bold naturalism, spontaneous modelling, a decorative subject and formal qualities. The human figure remains the main vehicle of expression; and abstract concepts are represented through personification.

Fred emigrated to Canada in 1913, settling in Toronto where he worked as a model maker and began work on his sculpture. Fred continued to sketch and sculpt and quickly became integrated within Toronto's small but active sculptural circle. He shared a studio with a few other Toronto sculptors, including Margaret Scobie. Indeed, a number of his earliest sculptures done in Canada were of fellow artists, such as Walter R. Duff, Lorna Reid, and his future wife, Louise Brown.

In 1915 Fred participated in an important exhibition of Toronto sculptors, held at the Art Museum of Toronto (today, the Art Gallery of Ontario), which showcased the work of some of the most active sculptors of the time, including J. Lisney Banks, Emmanuel Hahn, Alfred Howell, Winnifred Kingsford, Edgar Laur, Frances

Loring, Bessie Muntz, Marcel Olis, Beverly Robinson, Lady Ross (Mildred Peel), Mabel Stoodley, and Florence Wyle.

This was Fred's first showing of his work since his emigration to Canada. He chose to exhibit three works: "Beethoven," "The Siren," and "Head (Sleep)." Reviews of the show were positive, and Fred's work, in particular, was described in a few of the newspaper reviews. On Fred's plaster relief of Beethoven, one journalist commented: "Something more than a portrait is Mr. Coates' relief of the great composer, who during his last years was shut out from all sound. *God's harmony thy prayer has satisfied, His music on thy listening ear hath rolled.* The massive head and lowering brows tell something of the artist's fierce temperament – power". The small sculpture, "The Siren," was described as "a whimsical idea well carried out ... which has grace and swing in the floating figures." Another journalist for the *Mail and Empire* described the same work as "an odd little piece that shows an imaginative artist ... filled with action and conveys the idea in a manner that is vivid, though impressionistic."[1]

At the outbreak of World War One, it is unlikely Fred received any official war art commissions. He decided, however, to use his artistic skill for the war effort by creating a number of designs for honour rolls. At that time many business firms in Toronto and elsewhere formed honour rolls of their employees who had enlisted in the services, placing them in prominent positions where they would have been seen by everyone. Fred designed an honour roll of his own in the form of a sculptural relief, entitled "For King and Country" which represented a Canadian soldier gleefully saluting the quickly advancing Victory, represented by a female figure. In the centre are the names of the recruits on a bronze plate with the caption, "For King and Country."

On 1st August 1916, Fred enlisted as a private (no. 527951) in the No. 2 Canadian Army Medical Corps as part of the Canadian Expeditionary Force, serving in England at the Ontario Military Hospital at Orpington, at the Westcliffe Eye and Ear Hospital at Folkestone, and at the Queen's Hospital in Sidcup. During his time in the Medical Corps, Fred turned his modelling ability from statuettes to soldiers, whose faces had been disfigured by shrapnel. In conjunction with the British Medical Corps, he studied photographs of patients before and after they had been wounded, and constructed plaster models to scale. One journalist recounted the painstaking process: "The plastic surgeons followed these forms minutely as they twisted human flesh into new noses and jaws. Dozens of operations were often required on one man, and all the time Frederick Coates acted as the 'facial architect.' The doctors knew how to graft flesh and bones; Coates knew what a remodelled face should look like."[2]

During his spare time, Fred continued to sketch and draw, often recording fellow servicemen and women at rest or play. He also contributed cartoons for an army publication satirizing military life. Whenever possible Fred would visit local sites and galleries. He admired the work of the British painter, G. F. Watts whose work he saw at the Watts Picture Gallery in Compton in Surrey, England. He also made watercolour sketches of some of Rodin's sculptures.

From his visits to galleries and sites, Fred collected postcards of paintings and buildings which interested him. The postcards of Lord Leighton's "Captive Andromachi" (in the Manchester Art Gallery), H.T. Wells' "Victoria Regina," and Gabriel Dante Rosetti's "Rosa Triplex" (both in the Tate Gallery), reflected Fred's interest in Pre-Raphaelite and Romantic Classical British painting. His postcards of contemporary English architecture, especially those from his native Nottingham, such as the Arch of Remembrance, the New Exchange Building, the New Market Square, and the East Midlands University, reflect his interest in Beaux-Arts architecture and monuments.

Towards the end of the War, Fred travelled to France, where he visited medieval abbeys, cathedrals and churches in Peronne, Reims, Amiens, Arras, Mons and Boulogne. He then travelled to London, where he made watercolour and pencil studies of historical objects and textiles at the British Museum and the Victoria and Albert Museum. After a short visit to his family in Nottingham, he was discharged from service in August 1916, and returned to Canada. After working for a short period in Ste. Anne de Bellevue, Quebec, he returned to Toronto, where he lived for the rest of his life. On his return to Toronto, Fred applied for a number of jobs, including a position as an instructor of art and design at the Central Technical School in Toronto. Eventually, he managed to get some work doing cover designs for the Canadian Academy of Music and for the Superior Restaurant in Toronto.

Between 1915 and 1923 Fred exhibited his sculptures in Toronto at the Ontario Society of Artists (OSA), and at the Royal Canadian Academy of Art (RCA). In his solo and group exhibitions, Fred showed chiefly portraiture. His works included busts of the sculptor Margaret Scobie (exhibited at the OSA in 1917), his future wife Louise Brown (exhibited at the OSA in 1921), the artist Lorna Reid (exhibited at the OSA in 1922), and Captain Walter R. Duff (exhibited at the RCA in 1919).

During the period between 1923 and 1930 Fred Coates also regularly exhibited his designs at the Society of Graphic Arts, the Canadian National Exhibition and at Hart House in Toronto. "The Dream" (painted circa 1919), and "The Blue Plate" (exhibited 1923), are fine examples of Fred's growing confidence in the graphic arts. During this time he also designed and exhibited batik work, an art form which enjoyed a revival during the 1910s and 1920s.

On 22 June 1922 Fred Coates and Louise Brown were married in Toronto. Little is known about Louise's early life. She was born 21 April 1889 in Whitby Township, Ontario, the daughter of Hiram James Brown (c. 1853–1928), and Ella Leata Hoitt (c. 1868–1929), both of Whitby Township. At the time of his marriage in 1885 Louise's father was a telegraph operator in Whitby Township. By the time of Louise's birth, four years later, he had become a cloth cutter.

Soon after Louise was born, the family moved to Toronto, settling in Parkdale. In 1891 they were living at 40 Gwynne Avenue in a relatively new house in a middle-class neighbourhood which included railway operators, dressmakers, carpenters, shipping express agents, and clerks. Hiram Brown first worked as a cutter in James W. Isaac's Merchant Tailor shop at 1382 Queen Street West in Toronto. By 1896 he opened up his own tailor's business out of a shop across the street from his former employer on Queen Street West, and in the same building where the family also lived. The family moved a few more times on Queen Street West, always living and working out of the same building. In 1921, however, Hiram Brown separated the business office from his residence, and the family moved to 146 Springhurst Avenue in Toronto.

An artist in her own right, Louise was a talented painter who studied under J. W. Beatty (1868–1941) and graduated from the Ontario College of Art in Toronto. A number of paintings, now in private collections, reflect Beatty's influence in Louise's landscape painting and technique. She was good friends with the Toronto sculptors Frances Loring (1887–1968) and Florence Wyle (1881–1968), and evidently shared a studio with them at one time.[3] One of the earliest photographs of Louise illustrates a trip she took to Washington in March 1913 with a few of her friends, one of them being Frances Loring.

Around 1917 she participated with Loring and Wyle in an exhibition at the Women's Art Association, showing thirty-nine of her works. Three of her oil sketches, "Stepping Stones," "Drifting Clouds" and "Watery Sky," were pointed out by one reviewer as being particularly worthy of mention, and were described as "quite unpretentious as to size" and being "very delightful and spontaneous." During World War One, she worked out of a studio located at 600 Sherbourne Street in Toronto, and which was nicknamed the "Red Barn." Although she was primarily a painter, during the war she worked on a major sculptural commission and, in 1917, exhibited a bust of a girl's head at the Royal Canadian Academy.

Louise was a versatile artist and also practiced weaving, jewellery-making, basketry, pottery, bookbinding, as well as linoleum- and textile-block printing, and stencilling. She exhibited her textile and needlecraft work and one year, at the Canadian National Exhibition in Toronto, Louise demonstrated block printing on textiles and paper, and displayed examples of her bookplates and pointed scarves.[4] Avid photographers, Fred and Louise exhibited their photography in local exhibitions. Their talents as artists, Fred, largely in sculpture and modelmaking, and Louise, in painting and crafts, would come in useful in one of their biggest undertakings – the building of their home "Sherwood."

NOTES

1. "Local Artists Show Sculptory" *Mail and Empire* (27 November 1915).

2. "Man Who Makes Colours Do Strange Things", *Toronto Star Weekly*, (18 April 1934).

3. The best account of Loring and Wyle is contained in Christine Boyanoski's *Loring and Wyle: Sculptors' Legacy* (Toronto: Art Gallery of Ontario, 1987)

4. "Needlecraft at the Exhibition" in an unidentified newspaper clipping, Frederick Coates scrapbook, University of Toronto Archives.

Fred sculpting a portrait bust of fellow sculptor,
Margaret Scobie (ca. 1915).

Left: *Bas-relief of Walter R. Duff (exhibited 1919).* Below: *Mantel of the* Death of Socrates *(circa 1912).*

Private Fred Coates with plaster casts.

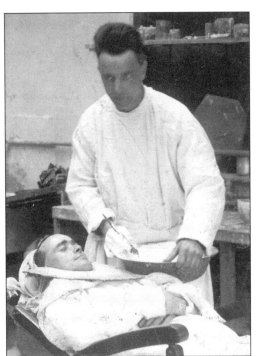

Fred demonstrating the art of plaster casting (ca. 1917-19).

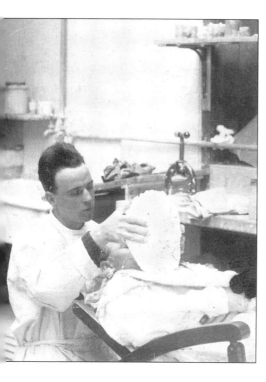

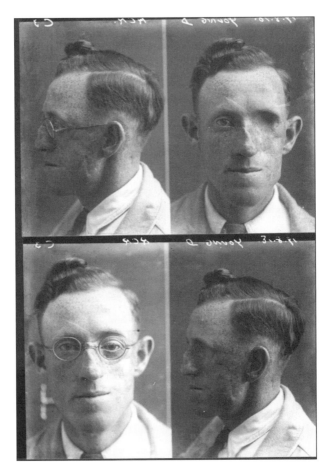

A soldier demonstrating the use of a prosthetic eye made by Fred (1918).

Left: *Louise in her studio, The Red Barn.* Below: *Louise's oil sketches.*

The construction of Sherwood,
the Coates house on Chine Drive in Scarborough.

Revisiting Sherwood

PAUL MAKOVSKY

I taught art before we were married, but afterward stayed in the house. Everything we had went into it.

Louise Coates

AFTER FRED COATES RETURNED TO Canada from overseas, he used Louise Brown's Sherbourne Street address as his mailing address for a short time, before moving to West Hill, Ontario (now part of Scarborough), where he remained for a year or so.

In 1919 Fred and Louise began work on one of their most important projects – the design and construction of their home, on the wooded ravine overlooking the Scarborough Bluffs. With the assistance of a carpenter, a stonemason and neighbours, they constructed the whole of this medieval-style house, complete with secret passage, which was described by a journalist at the time as "one of the most romantic houses in Canada.... It might be called a magic house, for if the exterior is changeless, the interior is as flexible as Mr. Coates' accomplishments and stage settings."

Fred had purchased a large wooded lot in Scarborough [plan 1566, lot 434] from the owner of a neighbouring lot, George Giesecke (1888-1976), a landscape artist, whom he had met at an artist's party before World War One. Only those trees needed for the construction of the house were cut down. The land in and around Chine Drive had been purchased around 1911 by Cecil White, a

Toronto real estate developer, who had plans to develop the land into a suburban community.[1] A few of the lots were purchased from White before the outbreak of World War One, but it was only after the end of the War, when the majority of the lots on the street were sold that owners began building residences on the land. White had purchased the land from the Ashbridge family, descendants of Sarah Ashbridge, one of Scarborough's pioneer settlers who, in 1799, was granted 300 acres extending north from the bluffs east of Midland Avenue in Scarborough.[2]

The style of the Coates house derived from the English medieval vernacular cottage, popularized by British artists and architects, such as William Morris (1834–1896) and Philip Webb (1831–1915), of the Arts and Crafts period, of the late nineteenth century. The Arts and Crafts movement revived the vernacular forms of English rural domestic architecture, and was an architectural aesthetic rather than an architectural style. The movement found supporters in North America, where nostalgia for the past and an admiration for things British fostered the transatlantic development of this revival. By the end of World War One, the style took hold in North America, recalling the use of hand-craftsmanship and local materials and the ideal of integrating the arts into everyday life.[3]

Fred was certainly aware of the Arts and Crafts movement and its philosophy. While in the army, he visited old cottages in Petworth and the Old Town in Folkestone, which were good examples of picturesque medieval villages. More importantly, when he was stationed near Surrey, he visited the Compton Cemetery,

Watercolour sketches for stained glass windows by Fred Coates
(ca. 1919).

Mermaid, *watercolour sketch for a
stained glass window by Fred Coates (ca. 1919).*

Opposite top: The Blue Plate, *tempera on paper by Fred Coates
(first exhibited in 1923). Collection of Dr. Thomas Howarth.*
Below: *One of Fred's sketch designs from the series*
Dawn, Day, Dusk, Night *(ca. 1920).*

Skating costume designs by Fred Coates
(ca. 1930s).

Top: Clowns, *theatre set design by Fred Coates (undated).*
Collection of Dr. Thomas Howarth.
Below: Pool of Heart's Desire, *theatre set design by*
Fred Coates (ca. 1925).

Top: Geometric Mountains, *theatre set design.*
Below: The Cherry Orchard, *theatre set design*
(ca. 1925-1926).

Top: *Oriental theatre set design (undated)*.
Below: *Butterfly skating costume and set design
(1936). All by Fred Coates.*

Top: Hosta, *gesso on wood panel (1956)*.
Below: Flower Garden, *gesso on wood panel (1961)*.
Collection of Dr. Thomas Howarth.

Chapel and Cloister (built 1896-1906), which was decorated by the Compton Pottery, a women's Arts and Crafts guild directed by Mary Watts, the wife of the painter G. F. Watts. In his army notebook, kept while stationed at the Queen's Hospital in Sidcup, he clipped out an advertisement for "The Studio Yearbook of Decorative Art" (1919), a publication which featured some of the very best examples of Art Nouveau and Arts and Crafts designs. Moreover, during the planning phase of the construction of the house, Fred and Louise clipped articles and images from contemporary architectural periodicals such as *House and Gardens*, and *Beautiful Homes*, which featured examples of Arts and Crafts houses built in Britain and North America. By the early twenties, many of the homes in these magazines had been built for wealthy American industrialists.

In the spirit of the Arts and Crafts movement, Fred designed the house himself. A simple and unpretentious plan, the storey and a half house was built in a T-form with a steeply gabled roof. The main entrance is at the north side of the house in a small round tower, tucked between the front and back sections of the T. The interior was composed, on the ground floor, of a kitchen which boasted an array of shining copper vessels, a dining room, and a large studio. On the top floor, were two bedrooms which were tiny replicas of medieval palace bed-chambers. Finally, there was the bathroom – an aquarium-like room in which there were mermaids and fish constructed in relief so that one feels submerged in water when one steps inside. Fred also designed and crafted an enormous stained glass window for the facade of the house, which was lit by a spotlight from within and greeted visitors as they drove in at night. A wooden garage was also built next to the house. Louise used the top floor as her studio, where she practiced her weaving and painting.

The house was named "Sherwood," and medieval references were found throughout in its design and decoration. The tower, which served as one of the entrances, contained two narrow windows of heavily leaded, richly coloured stained glass. The floor of the entrance to the house was decorated with a tulip motif, made of stone pebbles set in concrete. The newel post and railings were whimsically decorated with a bird's nest, a beautifully hand-carved wooden owl and squirrel.

Around 1930, when they had more income, Fred and Louise began adding more medieval designs to the house. In the dining room, for example, the walls were decorated in gold leaf, and painted with vibrant figures of characters from the various plays he produced at Hart House, and an intriguing map of Sherwood Forest. (Fred, it will be remembered, was born in Nottingham, the birth-place of Robin Hood.) Fred also sculpted two stone monks – one drinking ale, another praying – in stone brackets which support the beamed ceiling of the dining room.

To enhance the decor of the house, Fred designed two large-size carved and coloured linoleum panels measuring about eight feet wide by four feet in height; the first depicts a female figure in a garden; the other depicts medieval minstrels. These panels, created in 1930, hung in the studio of the Coates home for many decades, and added to the medieval character of the house. Beside the medieval motifs of the decoration, the Coates also used modern objects as they saw fit. Diane Layng, who as a child visited the house in the forties, remembers the brightly coloured Fiestaware which was displayed upright on the open shelves. In another example, Louise decorated a medieval-style chair with a seat cushion covered with one of her bright and colourful abstract geometrical patterns.

The handcrafted quality of many objects in the house was in keeping with the overall Arts and Crafts aesthetic. Wardrobes and corner cupboards were hand crafted by either Fred Coates or by neighbours, and were decorated with naturalistic designs. Ornamental iron work, such as hinges, latches, brackets and door knockers, were designed and crafted by the Canadian Ornamental Iron Company of Toronto, a small foundry which specialized in hand-made but commercially bought fittings. A spinning wheel which originally stood in the living room and studio harkened back to a nostalgic past, but at the same time served as a utilitarian tool for Louise in the preparation of her weaving. Louise designed and bound in leather a guest book. Its cover, done in Old English script, is adorned with acorns, an owl and a squirrel motif which are found in decorations elsewhere in the house. Other naturalistic motifs, such as hostas, cosmos, and acorn leaves, all found in the neighbourhood, provided Fred with inspiration for the design of a number of painted gesso panels.

The aim of creating harmony with the past also extended beyond the confines of the house itself. Many Arts and Crafts practitioners created a formal garden to balance the "natural" house. The aim, as one British Arts and Crafts architect wrote, was to provide "a sunny wall, a pleasant shade, a seat for rest, and all around the sense of the flowers, their brightness, their fragrance." The textural qualities and colour of materials (whether shrubs and plants, or stone and brick) were emphasized through geometric, controlled organization. The Coates' storybook house included a sunken garden designed by Fred as well as a trellis filled with roses, a reflecting pool and a whimsical fountain. Moreover, Fred and Louise used local animals, such as squirrels, owls and birds, as inspiration for their designs.

The Coates' studio is perhaps the most splendid room in their magnificent dwelling. Shortly after the house was completed and the Coates were settled in, the space was primarily used as a working studio where Fred worked on his sculptural projects. Although it was nominally a timbered room, the Coates delighted in turning the room into anything from a circus ring to a cowboys' camp. One day it would be an old world church with a massive nailed gate; another week it would be a bazaar or a Spanish grandee's apartment.

Fred and Louise entertained frequently, and for over three decades the couple were well known for their masquerade parties, charades, and the musical and theatrical performances staged at their house. The themes of their parties varied and visitors would dress for entertaining events such as an Elizabethan evening or a night of Ali Baba and the Forty Thieves. For their Spanish masquerade the Coates received guests in Spanish costume, Louise in a striking white gown. The thirty-six guests were also in Spanish costume, and the Spanish theme was cleverly maintained in decorations, dinner and music.

A newspaper journalist, discussing Fred's work, described another of the parties:

And speaking of him [Fred Coates] reminds us of the truly gorgeous Elizabethan party at their home in Scarborough, to which fifty or more of Mr. and Mrs. Coates' friends, mostly artists of some kind, were bidden not so long ago. These two splendid craftsmen, for Mrs. Coates is as clever an artist as her husband, had transformed their fine studio into an Elizabethan interior for the occasion. When guests arrived in costumes authentic of the period – gay ladies in colourful brocades and lace, cavaliers in velvet and plumed hats, slim youths in doublet and hose with the Church represented by a cardinal, a nun and a friar – and dancing took place on the flag-paved floor to music coming from the musician's gallery and the guests moved in the soft glow of light filtering through the stained glass (parchment!) windows, the scene was amazingly beautiful.[4]

For over four decades a steady stream of well-known Torontonians visited Fred and Louise Coates at their house. They included Vincent and Alice Massey; theatre directors Bertram Forsyth and Boris Volkoff; artists Charles Jeffreys, Yvonne McKague Housser, Dorothy Stevens, Frances Loring and Florence Wyle; and architects Edward Carswell, Harland Steeles and Eric Ross Arthur.

The Coates's connection with many artists, both on Chine Drive and elsewhere in Toronto, suggests a formal artist colony of some sort. Although this is unlikely, there was reference to the existence of one group. In 1922, shortly after the Coates had settled in the Chine Drive community, Fred Coates made some rough design sketches above which he printed the words "Beechgrove Crafts." Later that same year in her Christmas card to the Coates, their neighbour, Anne Giesecke, made reference to the "Beech Grove Group." Later, by virtue of the exhuberant parties, the individuality of the neighbouring houses and the eccentricity of the inhabitants, the street became known as "At Oddity's End."

NOTES

1. For a discussion of Chine Drive, see Hrag Vartanian's "Chine Drive: An Arts and Crafts suburb and its context" later in this catalogue.

2. Robert R. Bonis, *A History of Scarborough* (Scarborough: Scarborough Public Library, 1968), p. 49.

3. A good introduction to the Arts and Crafts movement is contained in Elizabeth Cumming and Wendy Kaplan's *The Arts and Crafts Movement* (London: Thames and Hudson, 1991).

4. "An Elizabethan Party" in *The Curtain Call*, pp. 1-2, undated newspaper clipping, in the Fred Coates Scrapbook, University of Toronto Archives.

Sherwood, the Coates house on Chine Drive in Scarborough,
shortly after completion (ca. 1922).

Top: *A view of the Coates house, from the southeast.*
Below: *from the north (ca. 1922).*

Top: *The studio, fireplace and gallery.*
Below: *The studio, north window from the gallery.*

The Elizabethan masquerade party held at Sherwood.

Opposite: *The Spanish masquerade party held at Sherwood.*

Opposite and above: *Louise and Fred in costumes for their masquerade party, "Night of the Forty Thieves" (1925).*

Fred and Louise relax with friends in the Studio (1934).

Louise in the Studio (1970).

Fred designing a stage set model,
with his stage set designs hanging on the wall.

Performances

PAUL MAKOVSKY

FREDERICK COATES MADE HIS MARK in theatre design in Toronto with his designs for the settings and costumes of Shakespeare's *The Tempest*, which was staged at Hart House Theatre in 1922 under the director-ship of Bertram Forsyth. It was described as "the climax of the Hart House season that year." As Art Director of the Hart House Theatre at the University of Toronto for the 1922-23 season and again from 1929-35, Fred was responsible for many of the settings, costume designs, lighting effects and playbills for the plays put on during this period. He was not only responsible for some of the productions, but was also in charge of the theatre workshops, as administrator and designer.

Hart House Theatre was built and equipped by the Massey Foundation, under the direction of Vincent and Alice Massey, as a repertory theatre for the University of Toronto and the public. The first performance was given in October 1919, under the direction of Roy Mitchell, who later became Director of Art at the University of New York. Fred Coates was hired to work under the direction of the Theatre's second director, Bertram Forsyth, who had studied under several leading members of the English stage.

The Hart House Theatre was one of a number of "Little Theatres" which had sprung up across Canada, whose chief purpose, in a city like Toronto, was to create a lively interest in drama as an art, rather than as a commercialized form of entertainment. Many people involved in the movement believed the staging by amateur performers of worthy plays, by classic and modern dramatists, would lay the foundation of a more serious form of theatre. This in turn would develop a generation of Canadian playwrights.

The staging of the *The Tempest* in 1922 was a brilliant success for Fred, and one which was remembered in the press for years after. His creative costumes and innovative settings (some of which used his colourful batik work) were met with critical acclaim, and soon after he was appointed Art Director for the Theatre. For the 1922-23 season, the Hart House Theatre produced classics like Francis Beaumont and John Fletcher's *Knight of the Burning Pestle*, *Hippolytus* by Euripides, Lady Gregory's *The Dragon*, and Goethe's *Faust*. Productions ranged in style from Greek classics and historical dramas to contemporary comedies.

For *Hippolytus*, Fred took his inspiration in scenery, costumes and groupings from Lawrence Alma-Tadema, who at the time was considered one of the authorities on neo-classical painting. His stage set designs for Ibsen's *Peer Gynt* (1930) reflect the influence of the American illustrator, Maxfield Parrish, and his other work often recalled the styles of Leon Bakst, Erté and Aubrey Beardsley.

Unfortunately for Fred, a change in the Theatre's art policy in 1924 resulted in set design becoming a course at the Ontario College of Arts, under the direction of members of the Group of Seven. Nevertheless, throughout the 1920s Fred and Louise continued to work with other amateur drama groups, including the Players Club and The Ottawa Drama Theatre which formed part of the Little Theatre movement. Louise played an increasingly active role in designing and constructing the theatrical wardrobe for various productions.

Fred's productions for the newly created Margaret Eaton Theatre, under the direction of Bertram Forsyth, were especially noteworthy. His designs for the interior and exterior sets for Chekhov's *The Cherry Orchard* were described as "quite charming," and Louise's costume designs were seen as "authentically Edwardian."

Many of Fred's designs for costumes and settings were streamlined and modernistic and even verged on the fantastic. His settings for Leonid Andreyev's *Love of One's Neighbour* (1925-26), a satirical burlesque, were described as "futurist," while his stage settings for the *Wizard of Oz* (1929-30), and *Peter Pan* verged on the whimsical. Geometric patterns and shapes, including ziggurats and lightning bolts borrowed from antiquity, were transformed into emblematic icons and hieroglyphs that came to personify modernity.

Fred was one of the few Canadian artists who displayed theatre set designs at exhibitions in Toronto, such as the Canadian Society of Graphic Arts, and the Canadian National Exhibition. The set designs for *Summer* (exhibited in 1926), *Fashions* (exhibited in 1929) and *Clowns* illustrated the artist's modernistic sensibility. A number of stage set designs were also used for dance productions including *Fronds*, *Modern*, and *Up with the Curtain*. Between 1923 and 1930 Fred regularly exhibited the designs for many of his more modernistic stage settings, which earned him favourable press reviews and awards. Other stage sets exhibited include: *The Storm Centre, East, The Puppet Master, The Museum, The Mariner, Castles in Air, The Magic Flute* and *The Flame*. Figures in these stage settings were sometimes alone. In his design for *A Modernistic Interior*, Fred portrayed a woman in a sleek dress and cloche hat bearing modern and geometric patterns. As inspiration for his fanciful designs, Fred looked to fashion periodicals such as *Vogue* and *Harper's Bazaar*.

In 1929 Fred once again became Art Director at the Hart House Theatre and his set designs continued to receive praise. The set designs for the production of Arnold Bennett's comedy *The Bright Island* (produced in 1931) stand out to such an extent that Lord Bessborough expressed great interest in the setting during an unofficial visit to Hart House Theatre. One journalist commented that the stage setting was "poetic and brilliantly pictorial," and another reviewer described it as "a masterpiece of design, colour, and lighting" and the costumes as "brilliant."

Fred also designed whimsical costumes for plays and was involved in the various skating carnivals in Toronto, by designing costumes and arranging lighting effects.

For a decade, beginning in the mid-twenties, Fred became especially interested in the light organ, and built a number of experimental colour machines. As one of Toronto's first "colour musicians," Fred interpreted music with colours emanating from the organ he constructed in the gallery at the end of the studio. By means of more lighting machinery than was usually found in many large theatres, he projected an ever-changing pattern of rainbow hues on a screen. These diffusing tints were accompanied by music from an electric phonograph. He employed moving colour in a production of *Faust* at the Hart House Theatre and later, in conjunction with a performance by a symphony orchestra of the *Grand Canyon Suite*.

His interest in the colour organ culminated in a concert in March 1934 at the Eaton Auditorium in Toronto, in which Fred collaborated with the young diva, soprano Edythe Shuttleworth, in the staging of Toronto's first chromatographic song recital. Following her debut at the Hart House Theatre in April 1928, Shuttleworth went on to study under Mme. Donalda in Paris, and Maestro Binetti in Milan.

The production of this recital was rather unusual. One journalist commented that Coates "was utilizing every mechanical device possible from motion picture projectors, diffusers, floods, colour machines to the big square affairs that stand in the wings of the conventional theatre; and for background a white satin cycloramic curtain, because it [created] a translucent depth which gives the sensation of gazing through an open window at unlimited space."[2]

Before her performance on the opening night, Edythe Shuttleworth was careful to tell the audience that she regarded it as an experiment. The performance consisted of a series of short songs. Miss Shuttleworth stood centre stage in front of the piano, in the light of white or amber spotlights, while two colour-wheels, one on either side of the stage, threw a series of changing abstract colour forms on the white satin screen behind her. These forms were produced by light reflecting from prismatic surfaces. Using his colour organ Fred produced a whole range of colours, depicting various dramatic and spiritual moods conveyed by the accompanying music.

A certain tonality was established; nature songs used green-blue; songs of indifference, amber; the Horror aria, deep red; the songs of Death, green with some blue.

Within each group there was a varied colour arrangement for individual songs; occasionally there was a change during the song itself.

One reviewer commented: "Most brilliant success was the Verdi number ... Miss Shuttleworth sang the Verdi excerpt magnificently, and the most dramatic colour organ effects were produced, a triumph for Mr. Coates as well as for Miss Shuttleworth."

Some reviewers had minor criticisms and the audience response was apparently mixed. For example, at various points in the concert, the audience was bathed in green or red light; and the majority of the audience took it as an opportunity to read the program. The music critic H. A. Voaden, wrote that the concert was "novel and interesting, and suggestive of ultra-modern experiments such as the one Vladimir Durov is to make shortly in his "Theatre of the Five Senses."[3] Fred continued his experiments with the light organ at several productions at Hart House. His biggest audience was in a performance with the local symphony.

NOTES

1. The best account of Amateur Theatre at the University of Toronto is contained in *Dramatis Personae: An exhibition at the University of Toronto 1879-1939* (Toronto: Thomas Fisher Rare Book Library, University of Toronto, 1992).

2. Untitled newspaper clipping, *Mail and Empire* (10 March 1934), in the Fred Coates Scrapbook, University of Toronto Archives.

3. H. A. Voaden, "Chromatographic Art" in *Saturday Night* (March 1934), in the Fred Coates Scrapbook.

Costume design by Fred Coates for
Foreign Man *(ca. 1930s).*

Left: *Cover of* Science and Invention *illustrating a light beam piano (May 1926).* Below: *Fred's design for a colour light machine.*

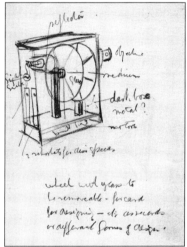

Opposite: (top) *Scene from* The Tempest *(1922), and* (below) *Scene from* Hippolytus *(1923) performed at the Hart House Theatre, Toronto.*

Fred's lighting and stage effect experiments.

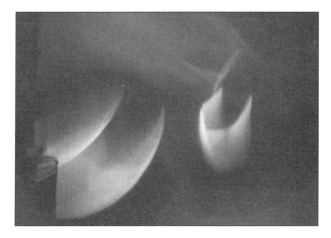

*Fred's experiments
using a colour
light machine
(ca. 1930s).*

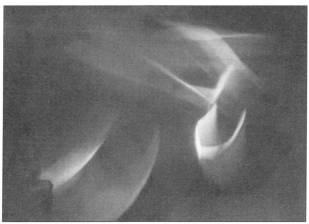

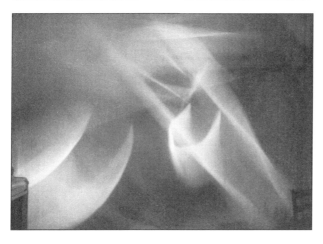

The design of the Hart House Theatre Mural illustrating Shakespeare's The Tempest *(completed 1934).*

The Stuff Dreams Are Made Of

PAUL MAKOVSKY

AFTER RESIGNING AS ART DIRECTOR of the Hart House Theatre, Fred Coates went on to teach model making at the School of Architecture at the University of Toronto, where he remained as a part-time instructor until his retirement in 1962. During World War Two, to help with the overseas war effort, Louise was employed at an aluminum factory in Scarborough. Little is known of Fred and Louise's artistic activities following the War. They continued, however, to be known for the parties and concerts given at their home, and Fred's only major project during the 1950s was the design of a number of religious plaques for a church in Toronto.

Fred's contribution to art and design in Canada is exemplified in a unique mural based on the characters and scenes from *The Tempest*, which is now situated in the lobby of the Hart House Theatre. Carved from a solid piece of linoleum and painted to give an effect of combining the best qualities of stained glass windows and worked leather, the mural took Fred two full summers to complete. During the summer of 1934, when he had plenty of free time, he made a working drawing and drew a full-sized sketch. The following summer he worked on the linoleum and finished the whole work by early October.

Fred based his images on various lines from *The Tempest*, and represented the various characters of the play such as Ariel, Alonso, Prospero, Caliban, Ferdinand

and Miranda. At the centre of his design Coates depicted Prospero, who speaks the line: "We are such stuff as dreams are made on."

Coates explained that he chose scenes from *The Tempest* because it was the first play he professionally designed. The play was directed by Bertram Forsyth and received recognition all over Europe. The Hart House Theatre mural in many ways is a summation of the work of Fred Coates. The panel evokes the various areas he worked in: stained glass, leather, engraving, architecture and sculptural relief. In many ways the work unites the various arts into a single art form, and at the same time memorializes an important moment in Fred's life – his first success as a theatre director.

Fred Coates died in June 1965; Louise died ten years later. Childless and hoping to keep the place intact, they left the Scarborough house and land in trust to the Board of Governors of the University of Toronto for the establishment of a scholarship at the Faculty of Architecture, with which Fred was associated for over three decades as part-time instructor in model making and art. Unfortunately much of the furnishings and art were dispersed at auction. The works which survive today in private collections and at the University of Toronto provide a glimpse into the life and work of these fascinating artists-designers.

There exists a fusion between the life and art of both Fred and Louise Coates. From Fred's career as a sculptor, theatre and costume designer, and from Louise's career as a painter and designer in many fields, their creativity is evident not only in their devotion to their art work and design, but also in their efforts to integrate their creativity into their daily lives. Fred Coates' interest in the theatre informed the design and construction of Sherwood and its ability to be transformed at the whim of its owners.

The masquerades, concerts and theatrical performances engaged their community in a spirit of fun and illusion and created an environment where friends and neighbours could partake in fanciful revelry. Through their life and their work, Fred and Louise Coates could justly claim: "We are such stuff dreams are made on."

Lot 434, the foundation of the Coates Chine Drive home.

Chine Drive:
An Arts and Crafts suburb and its context
HRAG VARTANIAN

THE CHINE DRIVE COMMUNITY OF Scarborough is a
small unique community virtually invisible to outsiders.
Even from the street the houses are obscured by large
trees or barely recognizable through the summer green-
ery. In the classic sense of the term, the Chine Drive
community represents a railroad suburb. The community
was dependent on the Grand Trunk Railroad which lay
to the north. Yet, by the time of the establishment of the
community the automobile had become an affordable
means of transportation and thus, liberated future
suburbs from a railroad umbilical cord.

A HISTORICAL VIEW

The suburban home is an expression of the family freed
from the corruption of the city and brought closer to
nature. Suburbia represents, *a collective effort to live a
private life.*[1] The European-style suburbs, which developed at the inner-fringe of the urban region, had acquired an unattractive reputation as the domain of
polluting industries, and ghettos. The Anglo-American
suburb evolved after access to the suburban lifestyle,
which at one time was the domain of the privileged, was
gained by the white-collar and the skilled blue-collar
classes.[2]

A desire to live within the vicinity of the urban centre
(for economic and social reasons), while simultaneously
being part of nature (for presumably physical and

emotional concerns) fuelled the exodus to less densely populated suburbs. The "city in the garden" was Chicago's goal after the Great Fire of 1871, and was its response to the juxtaposition of these two values. Slowly the culture and media responded to the demographic change – newspapers in Toronto and other cities featured "suburban news" pages started early in this century, while later television and movie culture further de-centred the importance of the urban core.

Suburban flight, in part, rejects the ethnic pluralism of urbanism and a community's need to maintain a static culture unspoiled by other immigrant customs. In Canada, the earliest suburban developments have been populated by those individuals who are part of the dominant economic or cultural groups. It is no surprise that the older suburbs of Toronto were predominately inhabited by British-Canadians. This was repeated in America where, according to Vance, the earliest subur-ban Anglo-American developments fulfilled a need to: "...maintain the distinctive [nativist] American culture that had emerged in the years between the War for Independence and the onset of the great immigrations of the 1840s."3

The development of packaged suburbs and the real estate agent allowed local covenants to exclude those members of society who were undesirable for a commu-nity. This practice was widely used in the Hamilton area at the beginning of this century. In the Hamilton region, Westdale's covenant featured this typical clause: "None of the lands, described ... shall be occupied by or let or sold to Negroes, Asiatics, Bulgarians, Austrians, Russians, Serbs, Rumanians, Turks, Armenians, whether British subjects or not, or foreign-born Italians, Greeks or Jews."[4] Different manners of racial covenants were fairly well established in many cities across Ontario, but did not have great popularity in the Toronto region.[5]

By the 1920s suburban development surpassed urban development across the continent, a dominance which continues to the present day.

THE GREATER TORONTO STORY

In opposition, but a party to the development of the traditional suburb, is the Arts and Crafts suburb. A number of Arts and Crafts suburbs in the Toronto region exist or have existed, populated by professional and amateur artists or artisans. These small utopian communities emphasized the individual as creator. *Wychwood Park* in Toronto still maintains its fortress-like independence and atmosphere of privilege. Started in the last decades of the nineteenth century it was conceived as an artist community and a refuge from the city.[6] In Etobicoke, *Davidson Crescent* had a reputation of being a winding hilly street where a coterie of arty people, painters, actors, musicians, and the like, inhabited the whole crescent.[7] Members of this community painted their homes with vivid colours and planted flowers throughout the crescent – illustrating a community's need for unique attributes which distinguish its members from those outside the colony.

An Arts and Crafts community represents a point of resistance against the traditional suburb. Their model was the medieval artisan, the inverse of modern alienation.

The suburb was initially developed in London during the late eighteenth century. Yet, the model had been adapted into North American culture so quickly that it is

assumed by many Canadians and Americans to have
originated on this continent. The rising middle class
sought to recreate the feudal, and idyllic communities
that were disappearing as a result of industrialization;
the utopian artisan community often saw itself as a
resistance against the disappearance of the pastoral life,
its greatest champion was William Morris and his brand
of middle-class socialism. While the English suburb is
dominated by the semi-detached house, the detached
bungalow dominated the aesthetic of suburban development in North America – both branches championed the
idea of *bricolage* and the "do-it-yourself" mentality.
Suburban development in the Toronto region parallels
the trends across the continent.

The public spaces in the suburbs are predominantly
commercial and characterized by consumer needs
(supermarkets, warehouse stores and shopping malls).
Suburbs often marginalize public space not bound to
commercial or utilitarian uses, thus, new types of
communal spaces are developed – often where access is
limited or purely symbolic.

THE CHINE DRIVE COMMUNITY

The utopian Arts and Crafts suburban colony exposed
more liberal ideals than the traditional suburb, and that
allowed the reinventing of individuals and their sur-
roundings. The topography of Chine Drive includes a
wooded ravine to the west which the southern portion of
the street follows to its terminal. The name *chine* in Old
English means "crack or fissure" and in an English
dialect signifies, "a narrow deep ravine or gorge." The
oldest residence in the neighbourhood is a white frame
farmhouse on the east side of the street which belonged

to the Saint Augustine's seminary (whose dome is visible from Chine Drive) and was given to the farmer of the seminary's fields upon his retirement. Noting this exception the east side was developed later and sold for residential use by the Seminary after the Second World War (circa 1948). Originally, the Seminary owned 141 acres in the area and it also sold land to the Scarborough Public School Board so that Chine Drive Public School could be built. Residents of the street who arrived after the war often had difficulty obtaining mortgages due to a belief that the land south of Kingston Road would inevitably erode into the lake.

The original plans for the Scarborough Bluffs development, of which Chine Drive is a part, date from 1911 and reveal a garden suburb plan [plan 1566, Metro Land Registry], with organic streets which close in on themselves and radiate towards the lake. But the present state of the scheme demonstrates the abandonment of the lower quarter of the plans, as a result of land erosion. Initially, Chine Drive was conceived as an outer boundary of the east and south regions – today the street abruptly ends at Bluffer's Park. Many of the early residents were amateur or professional artisans or artists, and the end of the street soon acquired a nickname, "At Oddities' End," a name invented by a local journalist who lived further up on the street.[8] In pioneer days the street was used as a logging road. At the turn of the century, the public would use Chine Drive as an access point to the Bluffs below. A number of the visitors decided they would like to live there.

The Chine Drive development included the restrictions of 50 foot fronts, and a green space between the homes. These regulations echo their nineteenth-century ancestor in Riverside Park, Illinois by Frederick L. Olmsted (1822–1903), which set the foundation for a modern suburban ideal. The regulations for Olmsted's general aesthetic included green belts between the homes, the exclusion of high walls, and a mandate that the homes be at least thirty feet stepped back from the sidewalk. The creation of the front lawn delineated a communal area, having the illusion of public space, but, in reality the space is distinctly private – the illusion is that of living within a park.

The Tudor and Elizabethan homes of Chine Drive signify the neighbourhood's desire to display attributes of common identity which hide in the dense vegetation, only the paved street (the first in Scarborough to be paved) crack the pastoral illusion. The emulation of another model of suburban community, whether Tudor, or Californian (both popular models in the twenties and since) evoke the ideals and aspirations of a community.[9] Yet, within the framework of the Chine Drive project individuality is encouraged and expressed through the home and its decoration. The Coates home has a extensive program of interior decoration and a large skylight which was not typical of Canadian homes of the period, but is part of the aesthetic of the Arts and Crafts style and its love of lightwells.

There is a very comfortable and enduring quality to the neighbourhood, particularly in Sherwood, where the hands of their makers are always present, and saturate the structures with social histories which are as interesting and enduring as the unique homes. The Chine Drive community lies in the serene setting of the Scarborough Bluffs and documents a community's desire to manufacture and celebrate itself.

NOTES

1. Lewis Mumford. *The Culture of Cities* (New York: Harcourt, Brace, 1938).

2. For a useful outline of the history of the American suburb, see "The Historical Evolution of American Suburbs" in Peter O. Muller's *Contemporary Suburban America* (Englewood Cliffs, NJ: Prentice-Hall, 1981), pp. 19-59.

3. P.O. Muller, p. 23.

4. J.C. Weaver, "From Land Assembly to Social Maturity. The Suburban Life of Westdale (Hamilton), Ontario, 1911-1951," *Histoire Social/Social History* 11 (1978), p. 421.

5. Ross Paterson, "Creating the Packaged Suburb: The Evolution of Planning and Business Practices in the Early Canadian Land Development Industry." in *Suburbia Re-examined*. Barbara M. Kelly, ed. (New York: Greenwood, 1989), pp. 119-32. Such clauses came under attack in 1945 when Justice Kieller MacKay at Osgoode Hall handed down a ruling that a restrictive land sale covenant which stated that land "was not to be sold to Jews or persons of objectionable nationality" was declared "void and of no effect." "Covenant Against Jew Buying Land Illegal," *Toronto Daily Star*, 1 November 1945, p. 1.

6. Keith M.O. Muller. *The History and Development of Wychwood Park: 1888-1918* (Toronto, 1981).

7. Esther Heyes. *Etobicoke: from Furrow to Borough* (Etobicoke: Borough of Etobicoke Civic Centre, 1974), p. 120.

8. Author's and Paul Makovsky's interview with Leslie and Bernice Campbell, 2 November 1996.

9. P.O. Muller, pp. 49-51.

Neighbours in Coates's dining room.

Top: *The Coates house, studio and garage.*
Below: *Fred and his car in front of his house.*

Fred and Louise Coates.

Chronology

1889   21 April
Ella Louise Brown is born in Whitby Township, Ontario, the daughter of Hiram J. Brown and Ella L. Hoitt.

1890   27 September
Fred Coates is born in Nottingham, England, the son of Frederick Charles Coates and Abigail Dexter.

1906
Fred receives a bronze medal for drawing from Nottingham High School.

1913
Louise travels to Washington with her friends, one of whom is the sculptor Frances Loring. Fred receives a bronze medal for a modelled design for a bronze panel.

1915
Fred exhibits three of his sculptures in a group show at the Art Gallery of Toronto.

1916
Fred exhibits a portrait bust in plaster at the Royal Canadian Academy (RCA).

1916–1919
As a Private in the Canadian Army Medical Corps, Fred is stationed at Folkestone, Sidcup and Orpington in England.

1917
Fred exhibits his plaster sculpture of Margaret Scobie at the Ontario Society of Artists (OSA) exhibition at the Art Gallery of Toronto, and also at the RCA in Montreal. Around this time, Louise, a graduate of the Ontario College of Art, exhibits 39 of her paintings at the Women's Art Association along with sculptures by Loring and Wyle.

1918
Louise resides at 600 Sherbourne Street in Toronto. She exhibits a plaster study of a Girl's Head at the RCA.

1919
Fred is discharged from the army and, after a short visit to Nottingham, returns to Toronto. He exhibits his plaster relief of Captain Walter R. Duff at the RCA. and is listed as living at RR 2, in West Hill, Ontario. Fred and Louise also begin the planning and construction of their house on Chine Drive in Scarborough.

1921
Fred exhibits his plaster sculpture of Louise Brown and a plaster relief of Lorna Reid at the OSA exhibition at the Art Gallery of Toronto. Fred is appointed to the Chair of Modelling at the Royal College of Dental Surgeons, Toronto.

1922 ca.
Fred is a Professor at the School of Practical Science at the University of Toronto.

1922   22 June
Fred Coates and Louise Brown are married at Parkdale
Methodist Church in Toronto.

1922–23
After designing the settings and costumes of
Shakespeare's *The Tempest*, for Hart House Theatre,
Fred becomes Art Director at the Hart House theatre,
designing that season's productions including: *Knight of
the Burning Pestle*, *Hippolytus*, *The Dragon*, *Belinda*,
The Witch, *The Rivals*, and *Orpheus and Eurydice*.

1923
An exhibition of batik work by Fred is shown at the Arts
Club in Montreal.

1924–30
Fred exhibits over 50 of his works including stage
settings, works on tempera, magazine covers and window
displays at the Canadian Society of Graphic Art and at
the Canadian National Exhibition.

1925–26
Fred and Louise work on productions of *A Kiss in
Xanadu*, *Love of One's Neighbour*, *The Cherry Orchard*,
and *Caesar and Cleopatra*.

1926
Fred wins a bronze medal and cash prize for the finest
exhibit in the design of graphic art at the Third annual
exhibition of the Canadian Society of Graphic Arts in
Toronto.

1929
Fred's sketches are exhibited at Hart House.

1930–35
Fred becomes Art Director of Hart House Theatre, overseeing productions such as *Make Believe, Wizard of Oz, Peer Gynt, Faust, The Comedy of Errors, Liliom, The Bright Island, The Man with a Load of Mischief, A Murder Has Been Arranged,* and *Good Morning Bill.*

1934
Fred collaborates with Edythe Shuttleworth in Toronto's first chromotographique song recital in the Eaton Auditorium.

1934–35
Fred designs and completes work on the Hart House Theatre mural. When finished it measures 9 feet wide by 12 feet high.

1930s–1962
Fred Coates becomes a demonstrator at the University of Toronto's School of Architecture, showing students how to build models.

1965   18 June
Fred Coates dies in his Scarborough Bluffs home.

1970
Louise Coates takes her first trip to England and visits one of Fred's sisters.

1975   22 July
Louise Brown Coates dies.

The auction at the Coates house in 1975.
Photo courtesy of Dr. Thomas Howarth.

PHOTO CREDITS

10, 60, 63, Hart House Theatre Collection; 12, photo of Fred Coates
by Ashley and Crippen; 28, 72, Pim and Debi Schryer collection;
39, 47, 74, Layng family collection; 56, *The Tempest* by
James and Son, Hart House Theatre Collection;
Hippolytus by Prof. G.R. Anderson; 59, Allan Sangster;
79, colour plate 3 (top), 5 (top), 8, Dr. Thomas Howarth.
All other photographs are from the Frederick Coates papers at the
University of Toronto Archives.

CURATOR

Paul Makovsky

ASSISTANT CURATOR

Hrag Vartanian

ARCHIVIST

Harold Averill

EXHIBITION INSTALLATION & CONSERVATION

Emrys Evans & Linda Joy

DIGITAL SCANNER

Maureen Morin

CATALOGUE DESIGN

Richard Miller

The typeface is Sabon.
One thousand copies printed by The Vincent Press Ltd.
Peterborough, Ontario
January 1997.